WOOLRICH
175 Years of Excellence

by
Doug Truax

CROFTON CREEK PRESS
South Boardman, Michigan

© 2005 by Woolrich, Inc.
All rights reserved. Published 2005
Printed in the United States of America

First Edition
10 9 8 7 6 5 4 3 2 1

Published by Crofton Creek Press
2303 Gregg Road SW
South Boardman, Michigan 49680
E-mail: publisher@croftoncreek.com
Web site: www.croftoncreek.com

Text design: Angela Saxon, Saxon Design, Inc., Traverse City, Michigan
Cover design: Rick Wattai, Threshold Creative, Inc., Lebanon, Pennsylvania
Printed by: Jostens Book Manufacturing, State College, Pennsylvania

Prologue

The 175-year history of Woolrich is in many ways a reflection of the same time period in our country's history. In 1830, when John Rich and Daniel McCormick established a partnership, which later became known as Woolrich, the United States was an agrarian society and north-central Pennsylvania was a sparsely populated area where farming and lumbering were the main occupations.

In the early years, the company's emphasis was on producing and selling woolen fabrics and some basic garments to the people of north-central

This gentle valley in the Alleghenies of north-central Pennsylvania has been the home of Woolrich for 175 years.

Pennsylvania who worked in the outdoors. In later years, apparel sales outgrew wool fabric sales as fewer people sewed their own clothes. With transportation improvements the company began selling garments and fabric throughout a larger geographic area, first regionally, then nationally, and today internationally. While Woolrich has always produced products for people who spend a great deal of their time in the outdoors, today it is more for people who spend their leisure time outdoors. As society changed, the company changed its product, but always with function and practicality in the forefront.

It has been my honor to be associated with Woolrich in one way or another for over fifty years. My family moved to Woolrich, Pennsylvania, from Rhode Island in 1953 when I was two years old. My mother was Catherine Rich Brayton, the daughter of Robert F. Rich, who was the great-grandson of the founder John Rich. My father, Roswell Brayton, Sr., had been in the textile business in New England when his father-in-law asked him to come to Woolrich to take a management position in the company. My grandfather Bob Rich had just retired from twenty years as a United States Congressman. Baba, as all of us thirteen grandchildren called him, brought my father to Woolrich to help modernize the woolen mill. My Grandmother Rich had died in 1951 when I was six months old.

My earliest memories are of growing up in the village of Woolrich where my father walked to work and most of my friends' parents worked in the mill. My cousin John William Rich and I used to sneak into the wool shed where huge 500-pound bales of wool were stored, and we would jump from one stack to another. It was hard for the watchman to catch us since we knew every possible escape route across the roof of the mill. As a young boy I remember almost constant construction going on as Woolrich expanded both its woolen mill and its apparel manufacturing facilities. I remember sewing plants being built both in Woolrich and neighboring communities of central Pennsylvania.

The company also acquired apparel plants in Colorado, Nebraska, and later Georgia. Woolrich the company was expanding very quickly in the 1960's and 1970's, while Woolrich the town remained a small, fun village to grow up in where everyone knew everyone. The company, with its manufacturing facilities in ten locations and four states, employed over 3,000 people and was known for efficient, high-quality apparel production. This was in post-World War II America, when the United States had become the dominant manufacturing country in the world. Woolrich was part of that U.S. industrial complex.

In the 1980's, U.S. apparel companies began producing less of their own product and importing more of it, but Woolrich remained true to its heritage and continued to run ten apparel plants and a woolen mill. By the 1990's it was apparent that we needed to change in order to survive. It was no longer possible to compete while producing nearly all of our product in America. During the decade of the 1990's, our emphasis shifted from manufacturing to marketing. While we had never compromised the quality of the Woolrich product, we had failed to keep up with the competition in marketing that product. Our jackets and shirts were as good as they had always been, but we didn't spend enough in the early 1990's telling our story and getting the message to the consumer. In the latter half of the 1990's, Woolrich made great progress in catching up to the fast-moving market-driven U.S. apparel industry.

As we moved into the twenty-first century, we took another step and have now become a lifestyle-driven brand. For the better part of two centuries the company has made products for people spending time in the outdoors. We have built a reputation as a company whose name stands for an outdoor lifestyle rather than just apparel for the outdoors. Our product offering now includes hats, gloves, socks, footwear, and accessories, as well as furniture and products for the home.

In 2005 we began operating our newest business unit, the Woolrich bottled water facility. We are now piping water from springs on our land to the bottling facility, a building that was originally built as an apparel distribution center. This is but the most recent example of the company's brand extension.

It is not possible for a company to keep up with this ever-accelerating pace of change without dedicated, intelligent, and hard-working employees. The celebration of Woolrich's 175th anniversary is a celebration of our employees both past and present. Thousands of employees have worked for the company since its founding, and it is only because of the combined efforts of all of

these people that we have been able to survive. There are many families, of which the Rich family is only one, who have had many generations dedicated to this company. This book is really about the collective efforts of all past and present Woolrich employees, for without them there would be no company to write about.

Roswell Brayton, Jr.
President, Woolrich, Inc.

Woolrich

A Great Journey

Early in the nineteenth century, a young man named John Rich II boarded a ship in Liverpool and embarked for the New World. He was just one of thousands of immigrants who would set out for the new republic of the United States. English, Irish, Scots, Germans, and other Europeans were looking for new lives, better fortunes, and the greater freedoms that this burgeoning democracy promised.

Rich came from a little English village situated in the heart of the largest wool-manufacturing region in the world. Indeed, he was the son of a wool carder, a man who made his living straightening or "carding" wool fibers prior to their being formed into long strands called "slivers" ready for spinning into yarn. In England, wool was the stuff of power and influence. It became such an important commodity that in the sixteenth century, Queen Elizabeth I required the nobility to take an oath to the Crown while kneeling on a woolen sack, to remind them that Great Britain owed its power and influence to wool.

John Rich II

Despite the primacy of wool to the English economy, the life of a lowly wool carder was anything but luxurious. No one will know for sure what dreams the young Rich dreamt on the ship that carried him from Liverpool to Philadelphia. But we can imagine that Rich, like so many other immigrants, hoped for a fuller and more rewarding life.

Although he had limited education, Rich may have dreamed of starting his own business, or perhaps the bug bit him later when he was exposed to the entrepreneurial fever that was seizing the new land.

What he certainly could not have envisioned was that his journey would result in the creation of a company that would prosper for nearly two centuries. A business created not long after the Revolutionary War would go on to experience the Civil War, the Great Depression, two world wars, and the Cold War. It would be there at the beginning of the Industrial Revolution in America, witness the amazing growth of American cities, and experience the movement of large numbers of Americans to the suburbs. Started when the country was comprised of only twenty-four states surrounded by vast tracts of wilderness, Woolrich was there when the telegraph was created, and it would be there, too, when the Internet was born and cell phones seemed to sprout from every ear.

All the while, the business would remain rooted in the rural landscape of north-central Pennsylvania, not two miles from where Rich erected his first woolen mill.

(right) Workers take a break on the porch of the original mill building at Little Plum Run, while socks dry on the upper porch.

▶ **1830**

The first Woolrich woolen mill is erected in Little Plum Run, Pennsylvania, during the administration of President Andrew Jackson. John Rich II travels from logging camp to logging camp selling fabric, socks, coverlets, and yarn from a mule cart.

Woolrich

Beginnings

The twenty-five-year-old Rich drew on his English roots to land a job as a wool carder in Germantown, on the outskirts of Philadelphia, in 1811. A few years later he rented a small woolen mill from Nathan Harvey in north-central Pennsylvania's Mill Hall, in what would become Clinton County in 1839.

By 1830 he had put away enough money to join partner Daniel McCormick in building their own factory along a small, picturesque brook called Little Plum Run not far from Mill Hall. The location must have seemed ideal. To the north rose the Alleghenies, where the melting snow pack, spring freshets, and underground springs rushed down the mountainsides toward the West Branch of the Susquehanna River. The river valley was dotted with small farms recently hacked out of the wilderness, many of them tending sheep and shearing the wool. The West Branch, in turn, provided transportation and access to cities like Philadelphia . . . and from there the world.

The original log house built by John Rich.

Water was one of the major forces driving commerce in the emerging nation. And in this rural part of Pennsylvania, commerce was springing up everywhere in the form of small crafts and industries tied to the land and its resources.

Rich and his partner built their three-story mill building using bricks made from the red clay found on the land. A dam and reservoir harnessed the water from Little Plum Run and provided power to run the mill. Inside the mill, they were able to convert the wool supplied by local farms into finished goods. The wool was washed, carded, spun, woven, and sewn to make woolen socks, yarns, and blankets, in addition to flannels and satinette.

As ideal as it must have seemed at first, the site proved a disappointment. Little Plum Run was simply too "little" to supply the power they needed. Rich and his partner looked for other locations. They hoped to move the mill a half-mile north to a site known as the Watering Trough, where water from Chatham Run was being diverted, but they encountered opposition from the owner of a gristmill on the same watershed who feared the water diverted for the woolen mill would put a crimp in his operation. Rich and McCormick, however, found the site they were looking for just two miles northeast of their mill. In 1834 they purchased a 300-acre tract of land in Pine Creek Township along the more substantial Chatham Run. The price was $600.

First, Rich built a sawmill on the land to process lumber for three log houses and the

New Life for the Original Factory

The original factory at Little Plum Run built by John Rich II and Daniel McCormick has been beautifully restored and now has a new life as the charming Little Plum Inn. Where mill workers once used water-power to produce woolen blankets and socks, guests now sleep in three sumptuous bed-rooms. The interior is bathed in light from the abundant six-over-nine windows that once provided light to the workers as they did the washing, carding, spinning, weaving, and fulling of the wool in the 1830's.

The steeply slanted floors of the second-story porches are a unique feature of this post-and-beam-built factory. They were set aslant from the mill's native brick-faced walls to speed the run-off of water drained from washed fleece and fulled woolens originally hung on the porches to dry.

new three-story brick woolen factory, which measured fifty-five by thirty feet. In 1843 Rich bought out McCormick, and by 1845 he was able to open the new mill as the sole proprietor. That building sits today as part of the group of buildings, homes, and community establishments that have become Woolrich, Pennsylvania.

John Rich II married Rachel McCloskey, the daughter of a local farmer, on November 3, 1825. The couple had fourteen children over the years, eleven of whom lived to adulthood. These four sons and seven daughters were the second of seven generations of Riches that lived, worked, and died along Chatham Run, and in the process created a unique and enduring American business enterprise.

A plank house was built to replace one of the original log houses that was destroyed by fire. This was the fifth house erected in Woolrich, according to M. B. Rich.

(right) The building in the left of this picture is part of the factory built by John Rich at the current site of the Woolrich mill. This scene was photographed about 1887 after additional buildings had been built. The wagon driver is the founder's son, John Fleming Rich. Standing in front of the company store is J. F. Rich's son, Michael Bond Rich, with his daughter, Jean Rich (left), and son, Robert Fleming Rich (right).

▶ **1835**
Samuel Colt invents the revolver

Land of Enterprise

"Americans are constantly driven to engage in commerce and industry," wrote Alexis de Tocqueville in the French visitor's recollections of his visit to America in 1831–32. "Their origin . . . social condition, their political institutions, and even the region they inhabit urge them irresistibly in this direction. Their present condition, then, is that of an almost exclusively manufacturing and commercial association, placed in the midst of a new and boundless country, which their principal object is to explore for purposes of profit."

During his nine-month tour of America, de Tocqueville spent much of his time in Pennsylvania, and he undoubtedly sensed the growing spirit of

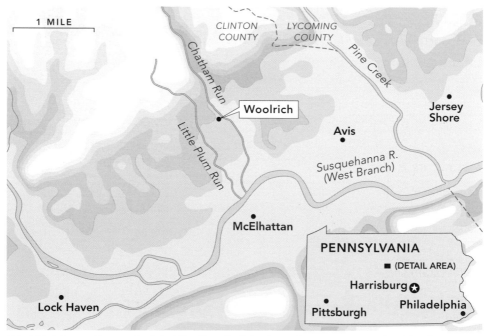

Woolrich is located just north of the West Branch of the Susquehanna River in the foothills of the Alleghenies.

Woolrich

American enterprise. America was electric with change. When John Rich II built his first mill on Little Plum Run in 1830, there were only two urban centers in the Commonwealth: Philadelphia, in the east, had some 80,462 residents with another 188,792 in the surrounding area; Pittsburgh, 300 miles west, had 12,568.

The rest of the state remained rural, populated largely by family farms. But in rural places like north-central Pennsylvania, capitalism and small-scale industry took root beside the family farm. New enterprises were being established by weavers, mill operators, potters, and shopkeepers.

Powered at first by the Commonwealth's abundant water resources, small mills sprung up everywhere. Farmers harnessed local streams to power an "up & down" saw to cut planks and shingles for homes and staves for barrels. Clover mills separated clover seed from the flower; fanning mills separated dust and chaff from grain; and feed mills ground grains for animals.

Loggers sorting logs on Pine Creek in the spring of 1908.

Spinning wheels and looms were standard equipment in area homes, but with the advent of mills like John Rich's, these cottage industries began to find a place in small, integrated factories in rural Pennsylvania. The mill John Rich established combined carding mills, which loosened and disentangled woolen fibers in preparation for spinning into thread, with fulling mills, which washed and pressed woven cloth to remove all remaining oils.

175 Years of Excellence

John Rich's first markets were close at hand—the lumbermen cutting the stands of virgin timber and the farmers tilling the land in the valleys. It was rough work that knew no regular hours and extended from the dead of winter to the heat of summer. Rich traveled from logging camp to logging camp selling fabric, socks, coverlets, and yarn to loggers from the back of a mule cart. The loggers' wives then made clothes from the fabric.

▶ **1844**

Samuel F. B. Morse demonstrates the telegraph to Congress

Logging began in the eighteenth century in Pennsylvania and reached its peak in the mid- to late-1800's. In the 1860's Pennsylvania was the nation's leading lumbering state. Williamsport, eighteen miles to the east of Rich's mill,

Reunited

As testament to the grim conditions that young John Rich II escaped in England, a letter arrived in the States from his father, John Sr. The year was 1838, and the letter was sent by the seventy-nine-year-old Rich to his grandson Joseph Hillier, son of John Rich II's sister Mary Rich Hillier. The letter was then forwarded to John II.

In the letter he explained that his wife had recently died after a lingering illness of fifteen months. "She and I in half starved situation having nothing to subsist on but the parish allowance which was five shillings week for us both out of which we have one-ninth shilling week to pay for house rent and fireing . . . My situation is most deplorable not being able to work . . . Please show this to your Uncle and when you write to me again give me his direction as I long to write to him, knowing he would relieve me in my miserable situation."

The letter, apparently, was in response to one sent by the grandson. But sending and receiving a transatlantic letter in those days was not an easy matter. "The letter we received was sent to your Uncle Stiles," the senior Rich wrote, "he was not at home. They did not take it in. The letter woman brought it to our house, I was not at home, as soon as I heard of it, having no money, I pawned my coat and got the letter, but have not had it in my power to redeem it yet." He adds that a friend gave him money to post his own letter in response.

The letter was forwarded to John Rich II, who was able to relieve his father's deplorable situation by bringing him to Pennsylvania, where he lived until January 7, 1847. It must have been a proud father, indeed, who witnessed the opening of the new woolen factory in 1845, seeing his trade as a wool carder come to such a rewarding fulfillment.

Woolrich

A Pennsylvania steam engine hauling logs to the mill.

supported a log boom that made it the lumber capital of the world from the 1860's to 1880's. The rafts of logs stretched for six to seven miles along the West Branch of the Susquehanna. In 1885, Williamsport's best year, nearly two million logs passed through its boom where they were then sorted and passed on to the appropriate lumber mills. Twenty-five sawmills produced 226 million board feet of lumber.

Just six miles to the west of the Rich mill, the nine major sawmills in Lock Haven were cutting 100 million feet of lumber per year. A local historian recalled that two sawmills near the small settlement of Jersey Shore (just east of the Rich mill) contained "sixty-four gang and English saws, with eight circulars. They were capable of making eight million feet of lumber per year . . . This was the most extensive lumber establishment on Pine Creek, and its site one of the best in the country."

▶ **1845**
John Rich's mill is moved to what is present-day Woolrich, Pennsylvania

175 Years of Excellence

On The Move

Pennsylvania joined New York in plunging the young country head-long into modern capitalism . . . With factories and canals, banks, and new efficient fuels, and especially the railroad, Pennsylvanians were the standard-bearers of a modern era.

PENNSYLVANIA: A HISTORY OF THE COMMONWEALTH,
edited by Randall M. Miller and William Pencak

The natural flow of rivers provided transportation for logs and power for mills. But nature was fickle and the industrious men and women filtering into

A canal boat carries passengers along one of Pennsylvania's many canals.

Pennsylvania and other areas along the East Coast were determined to find more reliable modes of transportation. First roadways were built, many following the old Native American paths. The state legislature chartered more than 200 turnpike companies to build more than 3,000 miles of roads by 1830. The network spread out like a web, connecting Philadelphia with the more remote parts of the state.

Canals were built beside the major waterways that crisscrossed the state, including the canal along the West Branch of the Susquehanna that reached Lock Haven in 1834. Canals allowed boats pulled by teams of horses to move lumber and goods more reliably and at less cost. They cut in half the cost of bringing lumber from Williamsport to eastern ports. Still, they were far from perfect. They couldn't be constructed across the mountains that angled across the state and they, too, became frozen and impassable during many months of the year.

So it was the iron horse—the steam-powered railroad locomotive—that would transform transportation in Pennsylvania and, for that matter, the rest of the United States. Rail lines began to poke into lumber camps. With rail lines, timber located farther from the major waterways could be exploited. At first the locomotives, in scarce supply, were used simply to take empty cars to lumbering sites. The locomotives returned empty, and the railroad cars, loaded with logs, used only gravity and the skillful hand of a brakeman to run the logs to the mill—a ride that would make today's amusement park rides seem tame.

Passenger rail traffic increased dramatically in the mid-nineteenth century.

Railroads continued to expand, carrying natural resources like coal, oil, and lumber, along with farm products, to the cities and bringing machinery and supplies to the country where small-scale industry

▶ **1846**

Elias Howe is granted a sewing machine patent

was flourishing. Passenger rail travel also sprang up. An 1837 advertisement boasted that the Pioneer Fast Line—using "splendid eight wheel cars" and canal mail boats called "packets"—could carry passengers from Philadelphia to Pittsburgh in three and one-half days. From there, passengers could travel by steamboats with the U.S. mail to Louisville, Natchez, Nashville, St. Louis, and other destinations.

Woolrich Railroad Vest

By the mid-1800's, Woolrich was making finished garments along with its woolen fabrics—largely due to the introduction of the sewing machine. As the railroads penetrated every corner of Pennsylvania, railroad men needed vests with watch pockets. Form followed function, and the Woolrich mill developed what became known as the Railroad Vest (it was first called the Utility Vest) out of charcoal-colored wool with a light gray pinstripe. The four front pockets provided a place to keep the universal railroad watch, plus places for tickets and other items. It wasn't long before telegraph linemen, lumbermen, hunters, and trappers discovered the vest as a great way to stay warm and have a place for gear.

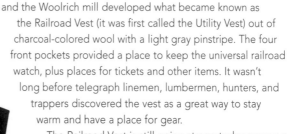

The Railroad Vest is still going strong today among a new breed of outdoors folks (it is now made for women, too) who find this compact, warm wool vest great for layering and carrying all manner of gear never imagined when it was introduced—from GPS units to iPods.

In the 1850's and 1860's the railroad network reached into areas around the West Branch of the Susquehanna. The Philadelphia & Erie Railroad reached Lock Haven in 1859 and the nearby town of Renovo was developed as a railroad maintenance center.

"When I hear the iron horse make the hills echo with his snort like thunder," wrote Henry David Thoreau, "shaking the earth with his feet, and breathing fire and smoke from his nostrils . . . it seems as if the earth had got a race now worthy to inhabit it."

The demands for labor to build steam engines and rail cars, lay track, and transport goods demanded more workers, many of them new immigrants. And the growing labor force needed clothing to keep them comfortable and well protected against the elements.

It was enough to make the wheels of commerce—including the spinning wheels at John Rich's woolen mill—turn. And that they did. In 1852 John Rich formed a partnership with his eldest son, J. F. Rich, and with John Colwell. The new partners each paid John Rich $3,666.87 ½ for their shares.

An inventory taken at the time showed a fairly substantial list of supplies and equipment that had a worth of $2,907.67 ½. It seems nothing was left unaccounted for, ranging from a clock that was worth $1.00 and a coal bucket and small kettle worth $1.37 ½ to the most expensive items—a condenser mule and spools worth $821.50. The fact

▶ 1848

President Polk verifies reports of gold in California

that accounts were kept to the half cent may give some indication of the parsimonious ways of the owner and his ability to stay in business while others failed. The valuation of stock was set at $11,000.95 and included over 9,000 pounds of wool, 111 yards of plaid flannel, 8 ¼ yards of red flannel, 193 yards of black casimere, and a host of other supplies and finished goods produced by the mill. Taken as a whole, the inventory provides an interesting view inside the process of making woolen goods in the mid-nineteenth century.

At the time of the new partnership, it was agreed "to the boarding of all factory hands and the price fixed is $1.50 per week for the hands, and $.12 ½ cents for every meal to be found and customers, horses or anybody in business belonging to the wooling manufacturing is to be charged, and it is understood all the girls boarding is to be $1.75 per week." It is not said why the ladies paid an extra $.25, but there was undoubtedly good reason.

▶ **1849**

Amelia Bloomer begins a reform of women's clothing

Buffalo Check Shirts were in abundance at this Pennsylvania deer camp.

Woolrich

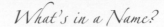

What's in a Name?

Among the earliest finished garments produced at the new woolen mill was the Buffalo Check Shirt. It was first produced in 1850 and was an instant hit with workers and outdoorsmen braving the elements in the expanding nation. Today, 155 years later, it is still going strong as a staple in the Woolrich line of woolen shirts.

Why "Buffalo" Check? The name seems to connote the wild open spaces of the West. But the truth is a little closer to home. It seems the designer of the distinctive pattern owned a herd of buffalo—nothing more complicated than that. The name stuck. And the shirt endured.

HISTORY OF THE
FIRST 100 YEARS IN
WOOLRICH

1830

70 Years Ago-1908

It was highly probable that Lock Haven would be represented in the arena at Wilkes-Barre if the spirit manifested at the preliminary meeting at the Presbyterian Chapel could be taken as criterion. The following singers were enrolled: Mrs. E. F. M Stevenson, Miss Sara Peck, Mrs. W. H. Stevenson, Miss Anne Bickford, Miss Madeline Youngman, Miss May Schuyler Suiter, Miss Amy Rickard, Miss Anna Ray, Miss Mauzie Suiter Mae McGinness, Randecker and Miss Eva Stanbach Mrs. George was the accompanist.

F. Rich, of purchased a fine two age Co. of by the Colu the J. N. Hamilton. were the Getz Comp h class local agents ade a vehicles rd a county comm the trip to William use Lycoming Cou elling sanitary plumb unty and jail with a similar plumbing buildings here.

Community

Perhaps more by necessity than by design, the Woolrich mill developed both as a business and as a community. Tucked in at the base of the Alleghenies 209 miles from Philadelphia, it was situated in what was then a remote area of Pennsylvania. As the mill grew it needed workers, and workers needed somewhere to live, to shop, to educate their children, and to worship. Neither John Rich II nor his descendents appear to have set down any guiding utopian philosophy for the community. But what emerged over the years was as tight-knit and integrated a community as any master planner could have envisioned.

Michael Bond Rich (1855–1930), a grandson of the company's founder, recalled his early years in the community in his book *History of the First 100 Years in Woolrich,* published in 1930.

Woolrich continued to build homes and community buildings for its workers in the neighborhood around the factory. This photo, taken from the factory, shows the community as it existed in 1916.

M.B. Rich
From One Century to the Next

Many men and women of the Rich family have played key roles in Woolrich over the years. Perhaps none of them captures the spirit of the family enterprise better than M. B. (Michael Bond) Rich, whose life began beside a little nineteenth-century factory surrounded by a few log homes and ended as the newly incorporated Woolrich was well established in the expanding commercial world of twentieth-century America.

Born in 1855, M. B. raised six of his own children in the same log home he grew up in. When still in his early twenties, he became a partner in the company with his father, J. F. Rich, and his brother John Rich. The company was appropriately renamed J. F. Rich & Sons.

M. B. not only became the driving force behind many improvements in the business—including new machinery, expansion of the factory, and spreading the good reputation of the company—he also served two terms in the General Assembly of Pennsylvania from 1915–1918.

During one of his campaigns for the Assembly, the *Clinton Republican* noted that: "the firm of John Rich & Bro. [as it was later known after M. B.'s father died], of Woolrich, as well as that progressive little town, has been steadily building up under the leadership and business-like manner, and the high esteem in which he is held by the citizens of his community is a high tribute to any man. The wheels of progress as well as prosperity never stop at Woolrich, as the management always keeps large orders booked ahead in order to keep the woolen mills running to give employment to their large force of men."

M. B. was a tireless public servant as well as an energetic business manager. His many service and philanthropic activities included serving as a trustee or board member of Williamsport Dickinson Seminary (now Lycoming College), Lock Haven Normal School (now Lock Haven University of Pennsylvania), and Lock

The five sons of J. F. Rich,
from left: W. F. Rich, M. B. Rich,
S. E. Rich, John Rich, C. H. Rich

Haven Hospital. M. B. was also a stalwart in the Woolrich Methodist Church, where he was at various times Sunday school superintendent, trustee, steward, and teacher. He also represented the church on various boards and statewide functions and philanthropies.

His granddaughter Elizabeth (Ibbie) Bell recalls that "Grandfather taught the men's Bible Class for 25 years and after his death the 50 class members arranged for the planting of many evergreen trees on both sides of the road leading into the town of Woolrich." Today, the trees are 40 to 50 feet tall and make an impressive sight on the mile-long road into town.

The home of M. B. Rich was situated directly across from the mill.

"He rigidly followed the rules of the Methodist Church as practiced at that time. He did not dance nor play cards," Elizabeth wrote, "however, he didn't forbid his children from doing so."

When not away from home on business or community matters, M. B. liked to relax in his home library, where he had an impressive collection of books. He also collected a large assortment of documents, letters, photographs, and historical accounts that he later used to create the company's centennial history, *History of the First 100 Years in Woolrich,* published in 1930.

In fact, it was as the 75-year-old M. B. was returning from the printer with finished copies of the book that he was killed in a car accident. Characteristically, that same day he had just completed transactions on the purchase of considerable property for the expansion of Williamsport Dickinson Seminary. In his will, Michael Bond Rich left $40,000 of Woolrich stock to the employees and the community. The employees subsequently voted to sign off the shares as a trust fund, one-half to go to the Woolrich Community Church and the other half to assist needy families, providing scholarships and support to many other worthy causes.

Today the trees planted in memory of M. B. Rich line the entrance to the town of Woolrich.

M. B. Rich remembers the old log house in which he was born and raised—a house, incidentally, he continued to live in as an adult through the birth of his first six children while his parents moved across the street.

In the old home my brothers and I occupied a room over the kitchen under the roof where we could hear the rain drops pattering on the shingles. It was designed as a boy pen.

There was a fireplace in the dining room, where hung a large kettle. The beams in the ceiling, supporting the second story, were so low that it required stooping to pass from one room to another. The floors, always clean-scoured, were without carpet except in the parlor.

There were three rooms and a kitchen downstairs and three rooms and a loft or boy pen upstairs.

My parents boarded the men employed in and about the mill who were not living in one of the three other houses in the place and, to room these employees, a building was erected about forty feet west of his [M. B.'s father] *home over a large spring. The lower story comprised a spring house where milk was kept, also canned fruit and vegetables were stored and bees were housed. Later, in this same building, a store was started where such commodities as syrup, tobacco, sugar, mackerel, pickled and smoked meats were dispensed. The sales books of the time indicate that plug tobacco was the leading article sold.*

▶ **1857**

Elisha Otis's first passenger elevator clears the way for skyscrapers

M. B. recalls that just north of the rooming house was a walled-in spring where the drinking and cooking water was drawn. Below it was a ditch where "we boys were sent every evening to wash our feet from time we went barefooted, on or about the first of May, until late fall."

Woolrich

It was at this spring that M. B. nearly lost his life. It seems his father was hosting a barn raising. A large number of men were invited and, as was the custom, were furnished with their meals and a drink. "On account of rain on the day set, the raising was postponed a couple of days and the spruce beer which was prepared (for mother would permit nothing stronger) had acquired a potency not intended. As it was accessible to me, I drank quite freely and, when later on I stooped over to get a drink from the spring, I fell in headfirst and was too much intoxicated to get out."

Interior of the Woolrich church.

Fortunately, a woman assisting his mother came to the spring for water—just in time to rescue and then resuscitate him. He notes, sheepishly, that it was the only time in his life that he ever became intoxicated.

Which is indeed plausible. The Rich families were hard-working, God-fearing souls to whom the church was of paramount importance. M. B. Rich devotes a large portion of his centennial history to the establishment of the community church and its activities.

In 1857 a Union Sunday School was organized. J. F. Rich, son of Woolrich's founder, served as librarian, teacher, secretary, and treasurer, and the roll included J. F.'s three-year-old son, John Rich. In 1860, M. B. Rich and Joseph Rich joined the congregation.

In 1868 the first church was built on the site of the present Woolrich Community United Methodist Church at the corner of Park Avenue and Mill Street. One of the church's proudest accomplishments was the establishment

The Woolrich Community Church, built in 1907. This church, still in use today, is built on the site of the original community church constructed in 1868.

of the annual Children's Day, launched on August 18, 1880. Before the day ended, some 225 children gathered to hear recitations, sing hymns, listen to scripture readings, and witness "the alphabet in rhyme by twenty-six little boys and girls, the same singing one verse of a piece of music called 'On Jordan's Stormy Banks I Stand.'" Between the visitors' basket and selling the event banner, $9.67 was raised, bringing the treasury to $16.16. A proud beginning.

By 1886 the Children's Day celebration was attended by nearly 800 people. Coinciding with Independence Day, the crowd gathered at the church and marched together to the chestnut grove under a banner bearing the motto, "God Is Our Refuge."

The settlement at Chatham Run was first called Factoryville, then renamed Richville in about 1866, and finally Woolrich in 1888.

Chatham Run is also referred to in various sources as Chatham's Run and Chathams Run.

M. B. Rich recalls the event:

> *After they reached the grove all were comfortably seated to enjoy the sylvan shades of nature, enhanced by the touches of artistic hands in a beautiful display of moss arching, numerous flags, bouquets, flower stands, and as a representative of the old Independence Bell in front of the background was erected a farm bell, that, by some strange coincident, seemed to reveal nature sympathy [sic] with the American people by refusing to ring on that day.*

Perhaps the bell was reluctant to ring out, but the voices of the gathering were not so reticent. Numerous hymns were sung, recitations ranging from "Turning the Grindstone" to "Gambler's Wife" were delivered, and the day was pronounced a rousing success.

Certainly the bucolic community growing around the Rich woolen mill was not immune to the influence of the outside world. But events that were overtaking the rapidly expanding country may have been muted by the time they reached this little village and mill.

The bank panic of 1837 led to a four-year recession. In 1840 there were 409 chartered railroads in the country riding over 3,300 miles of track. By 1860 there were nearly 30,000 miles of iron rails stretching across the nation. In 1831, Pennsylvanian Cyrus McCormick invented a harvester that would both cut grain and toss it on a platform. By 1860, he was making 4,000 harvesters a year and the grain fields were replacing native prairies with increasing speed.

▶ **1861**
U.S. Civil War begins

Samuel F. B. Morse demonstrated his telegraph machine in 1844, and in 1856 the Western Union Company was established. By 1866 America and Europe were connected by a transatlantic telegraph cable. Under the banner of Manifest Destiny, America pushed west, adding territory that would become the states of Texas in 1845 and California

Today Woolrich makes blankets commemorating the Civil War period.

in 1850. Closer to home, Philadelphia had become the leading manufacturing city in the nation.

But by the early 1860's even the remote settlement around Chatham Run was touched deeply by national events. The rumblings of the Civil War could be heard in Factoryville. M. B. Rich recalls "an earnest controversy that occurred in the weaving and spinning room of the mill when the boys were discussing the enlisting for the War of Rebellion. George Farley, Henry Farley, John C. Young, and others who enlisted and those who refused. Some loud talk and countercharges were made. I also remember—toward the close of the war—going to Chathams Run Post Office at Charlton for the mail and the cheering that would be given when I brought news of a victory for our armies. I recall the death-like pall that come over us all when the news of the assassination of Abraham Lincoln reached us."

In the South, cotton was king, but the cotton industry was built on the backs of slave labor. In the major industrial cities of the East, large textile industries packed workers into less than ideal working conditions and labor unrest was not uncommon.

Blankets for the Union Army

When the United States was thrown into civil war, Woolrich had already been in business for more than thirty years. As young soldiers marched into battle at Bull Run and Antietam, at Gettysburg and Chickamauga, many carried Woolrich blankets for warmth and comfort. Woolrich blankets were there through the sieges of Vicksburg and Atlanta and were there when the war ended at Appomattox Courthouse in 1865. Today, as the only U.S. woolen mill still in operation that produced woolen fabrics for the Civil War, Woolrich supplies major film studios and re-enactors across the country with the same quality wool goods for uniforms and blankets.

Terms of the Trade

The language of weaving and textiles developed gradually over the seventeenth and eighteenth centuries and is passed on to us today. Although the terms and their meanings change over time, here are a few common ones. (As compiled from various sources in *The Weaver's Craft: Cloth, Commerce, and Industry in Early Pennsylvania* by Adrienne D. Hood.)

Broadcloth: Woolen cloth woven in a plain weave on a wide loom (fixed by a statute in 1465 as twenty-four yards long by two yards wide). After weaving, the cloth is fulled and shrunk to make it warmer and denser.

Cassimere (or casimere): Patented in 1766 by Frances Yerbury, cassimere is a woven twill made with a fine yarn and, unlike broadcloth, does not need to be fulled. It is thinner and lighter than broadcloth and has a fine finish.

Flannel: Made of loosely twisted woolen yarn and woven to create a soft white cloth that can also be dyed.

Plush: Made of wool with a pile or nap, this is wool velvet. Plush comes in all colors and was used for breeches, waistcoats, and winter jackets, as well as for furnishing upholstery.

Warp: All the lengthwise threads of a woven cloth.

Weft: All the crosswise threads of a woven cloth. Each weft passes through a warp shed (the opening caused by a sequential raising of some warp ends and lowering of others, which allows a shuttle to carry the weft thread through).

Woolen: Yarn or cloth made from wool that is carded (brushed and rolled so that the fibers are aligned at a right angle for spinning).

Worsted: Term used to describe both a yarn and the cloth made from it. The yarn is made from long-staple wool that is combed to align the fibers parallel to each other. Worsted cloth is generally light-weight with a smooth finish.

Growth

The Rich mill, however, continued to prosper, and the progeny of John Rich II continued to provide workers and management for the enterprise. Unlike the massive textile mills in Massachusetts or urban centers like Philadelphia, John Rich's mill remained a small, rural enterprise typical of other businesses launched in this part of Pennsylvania.

John F. Rich

The business took a step forward in 1857 when an agreement was made to divide the company equally between John Rich II and his son John F. Rich. The company was now to do business under the name John Rich & Son. That was one of several name changes that would be made as new partners, in large part relatives of the Rich family, were brought in as part owners. Other company names included John F. Rich & Sons; John Rich & Co.; and John Rich & Bros. The company was not incorporated until January 1, 1930, when it officially became Woolrich Woolen Mills. In 1988 it became simply Woolrich, Inc.

By 1881 the capital in the firm John F. Rich & Sons was established at $19,169.62. The partners were J. F. Rich and his sons John Rich and M. B. Rich. The business by then had grown to include "manufacturing woolen goods, and selling, and buying, dry goods and groceries, at wholesale and retail, and, shipping and forwarding goods to such points as may be required."

Throughout the 1880's and 1890's, company growth was steady but modest,

with capital gains that ranged from just under 4 percent to 28 percent. In only two years in those two decades did the company run a deficit.

As a sure sign of continuing business success, the complex of buildings surrounding the original woolen mill grew steadily after the mill was completed in 1845. First an extension and an ell were added, followed by a three-story store and storage building in 1883 (used today as an office building). That building was added on to in 1907 with what was designated as the No. 2 building, a large brick addition built by Sheridan Cryder. Over the next twenty or so years, the complex continued to expand until there were some eighteen separate additions or new buildings added to the complex.

Cryder was not only instrumental in construction of the commercial buildings; he, along with E. C. (Ellery Channing) Tobias, was largely responsible for designing and building some seventy homes in the burgeoning community, in addition to the church, clubhouse, hall, swimming pool, and miscellaneous barns and storage buildings.

Tobias had been operating a portable sawmill north of Woolrich, sawing lumber for C. H. Rich. In 1890 he came to work for the company, first sorting wool. He rose to become a foreman and then superintendent—as well as a member of the board of directors—until forced to take other employment for health reasons.

Rising through the ranks to positions high in the company was not unique, and M. B. Rich in his centennial book takes great pride in outlining the contributions of many of the early workers and managers who played key roles in the business. Notable among them was George G. Ohl, who started at the bottom and rose to superintendent of manufacturing. He was also a company officer and a member of the board of directors. His brother, Clarence W. Ohl, was foreman of the sewing department as well as cutter and designer of garments.

(left) On the right, the George Rich residence in 1915. Across the street can be seen the Woolrich community center and store. (right) The residence of Robert F. Rich.

Family members depended on each other for the quality of the product. William Englert headed the weaving department, where creating the perfect fabric was dependent on the work in the carding and spinning departments. Luckily, William could depend on his father, Adam, and brother Charles, who headed those respective departments.

As new members of the Rich family reached working age, they too were expected to start from the lower rungs of the company hierarchy and work their way into positions of authority according to their talents.

In addition to the continuous building and expansion of the mill and settlement around it, there were setbacks. Fire destroyed several early homes, including the original log home of John Rich II. Sitting at the base of the mountains and adjacent to the West Branch of the Susquehanna, the area around the mill was subject to the floods that periodically swept through Pennsylvania. On May 31, 1889, rain fell with a vengeance on western Pennsylvania, causing the huge earthen dam at Lake Conemaugh to collapse and release a wall of water downstream that killed more than 2,200 people in the infamous Johnstown flood. Over in north-central Pennsylvania, the folks at Woolrich were more fortunate, but the flooding there did manage to sweep away a cow barn and redirect Chatham Run. A major fire ripped through the woolen mill in 1901, gutting the main building.

There were the inevitable mishaps within the mill, as well. M. B. Rich says the most appalling accident he ever witnessed was in the fulling mill. His brother John was greasing a piece of overhead equipment when his shirtsleeve caught on a setscrew and wound his clothing around the shaft. "He caught a crossbeam on the top of the stocks," M. B. reported, "and held on until the shaft tore every stitch of clothing from him except his shoes. When he fell limp to the floor, completely exhausted, it seemed always to me a miracle that his life was spared."

The main building of the Woolrich mill was devastated by fire in 1901 and promptly rebuilt.

Woolrich

WOOLRICH WOOLEN MILLS
WOOLRICH, PA.

Making Wool

The process of shearing sheep and weaving wool fabric is a craft that has been practiced for centuries. At first it was a laborious hand process, but gradually throughout the eighteenth and nineteenth centuries mechanization was introduced that made the process more efficient. Still, the process of spinning and weaving wool has remained fundamentally the same. Here are the basic steps of making wool fabric today.

Shearing

The sheep is sheared with hand clippers or power-driven machinery. The dirtiest and coarsest parts are removed and the wool is then rolled up and packed in bales for shipment to Woolrich.

Blending

The bales are opened and different types of wool—from the U.S., England, New Zealand, and other parts of the globe—are mixed in the right proportions for the fabric being created. The fiber may also be dyed at this point.

Washing

Using warm water and soap, the wool is scoured thoroughly to remove dirt and grease. It may take four or five scourings and rinses to get the wool clean.

Carding

The wool is carded by passing it through a machine with rows of teeth that straighten and interblend the fibers into a flat band. If it is a worsted fabric, the flat band is combed to make the fibers lie parallel to one another. The band is made into a soft, loose cord that is wound around a large spool.

Spinning

The spool is set on a spinning machine, and the cords are fed through spinners that wind the cord on small spools or bobbins, giving it the twist and elongation that add strength to the yarn.

Weaving

Depending on the type of patterns and/or fabric required, the colored yarns are selected to be set up on the weaving machines. The yarns are woven together and the finished cloth is washed to remove machine grease and dirt from handling. It may also be dyed at this point.

Mending

The fabric is thoroughly inspected and skilled workers remove any knots and repair any flaws in the fabric.

Finishing

The fabric then goes through a finishing process that varies according to the type of wool being produced. For some fabrics a process called napping gives the cloth a soft, fluffy surface.

A young woman demonstrates the Woolrich carding machine used to loosen and disentangle woolen fibers in preparation for spinning into thread.

The End of the Frontier

In 1869 the golden spike was driven that joined the Union Pacific and Central Pacific railways to form the first transcontinental railway. It was now possible to travel from coast to coast without interruption. The gold rush that began in California in 1848 was winding down. Timber was being stripped from the land with a frightening swiftness, providing building materials for the burgeoning cities. Logging camps moved from Maine to Michigan and then to Wisconsin and Minnesota. In their wake they left only the stumps of the once giant virgin white pines. Soon the loggers would set their sights on Washington, Oregon, and northern California.

▶ **1869**

Union Pacific and Central Pacific railways join to form the first transcontinental railway

Up until the late nineteenth century, natural resources had seemed endless, inexhaustible. But as the pioneering days of the West Coast reached an end, a profound change was beginning to grip the nation. The outdoors and natural resources—once a source of hardship and survival—were becoming for many a source of recreation and solace from the increasingly noisy and polluted cities.

There was no magical moment when the change occurred, and it happened in various places and among different socioeconomic groups at different times. But the change was unmistakable and it had profound effects on companies like Woolrich. The rugged coats, socks, and breeches that once made a day's work in the lumber camps, mines, and railroad yards livable were gradually being made for people who went to the wilds because they wanted to go. Increasingly, these folks found recreation in hunting, fishing, camping, and hiking throughout the forests and lakes that remained unspoiled.

As sport hunters took to the woods for recreation, they were often outfitted in Woolrich woolens. At the time, the outfit worn here was called the Woolrich Big Game Hunter's Suit and was made of 30-ounce wool, lined throughout. Locally this outfit was called the "Pennsylvania Tuxedo."

On April 23, 1851, Henry David Thoreau addressed a group in Concord, Massachusetts, and summed up his prophetic vision in eight simple words: " . . . in Wildness is the preservation of the World." The wilderness was something to be appreciated, not reviled. Although for many years Thoreau's words remained known to only a few, the movement to protect, preserve, and appreciate the outdoors was taking hold.

The movement achieved tangible results when, in 1872, the United States created Yellowstone National Park, the first large-scale wilderness preserve stretching over two million acres of northwestern Wyoming. The next great wilderness area was preserved in 1885 when the state of New York established the 715,000-acre Adirondack Forest Preserve. New publications like *Forest and Stream* (1873) were created to cater to sportsmen and outdoor enthusiasts.

Out West, John Muir would sound a similar clarion call to the wilderness a few decades later. "Wild country, according to Muir, had a mystical ability to inspire and refresh," wrote Roderick Frazier Nash in *Wilderness and the American Mind*. And Muir found support across the nation. On September 30, 1890, both houses of Congress passed the Yosemite Act setting aside a preserve much as Muir had proposed. President Benjamin Harrison signed the legislation the next day.

▶ **1886**

U.S. Postal Service recognizes the town of Woolrich and establishes a post office with John Rich as Postmaster

Buffalo once roamed the western plains in the tens of millions. By 1889 there were estimated to be 549 left. By 1890 the frontier was, for all purposes, gone.

Americans began to explore lands that had already been conquered, if not tamed. "The average citizen could approach wilderness with the viewpoint of the vacationer rather than the conquerer," Nash wrote. "Specifically, the qualities of solitude and hardship that had intimidated many pioneers were

Woolrich

Theodore Roosevelt (left) stands with naturalist John Muir on Glacier Point above Yosemite Valley, California, in May of 1904. These two men were instrumental in the movement to preserve America's wild lands.

likely to be magnetically attractive to their city-dwelling grandchildren."

The notion of vacations was a new one in early nineteenth century America, and at first only the upper class had the time and money to enjoy them. But the rising prosperity of America led to a growing middle class during the last half of the century, and that middle class increasingly sought relaxation and relief in vacations. The first getaways were camp meetings held by religious groups, but increasingly in the last decades of the century, vacations involved travel to resorts in the mountains and along the seashore, and trips into the wild country with little more than a tent. The railroads, whose lines reached into more and more areas

▶ 1903
Wright Brothers' first successful flight at Kitty Hawk, North Carolina

Wear Woolrich Weatherproof Woolens

Established 1830
Woolrich, Pa.

Philip R. Goodwin

of the country, eagerly promoted travel and leisure.

Between 1880 and 1885 Woolrich began producing a full line of wool shirts, breeches, jackets, and caps, many of them undoubtedly to be worn by people using their new-found leisure to explore the outdoors. By 1915 Woolrich offered ladies wool hose and double-front "Mackinaw coats." Wool sport blouses, all-wool bathing suits, beach robes, and wool golf knickers were added to the product mix. A nation enjoying itself in the outdoors proved to be an even larger market for rugged outdoor clothing than the original market of hardworking loggers and frontiersmen.

Vacationers sought out lakes and beaches in the latter part of the ninteenth century. Tasteful swimming attire, however, required more than today's minimalist suits.

The movement to preserve wilderness and seek a healthy, invigorating lifestyle in outdoor recreation found no better champion than President Theodore Roosevelt. As president he instituted the first federal wildlife refuges, national monuments, game preserves, and conservation

▶ **1909**

Ford Motor Company mass produces Model T

commissions. He set aside 150 national forests between 1901 and 1909 that protected 150 million acres.

(left) This hunter, depicted in a 1930's Woolrich catalog, is more likely to be sweating from the close approach of the bear than he is shivering from the cold, thanks to his all-wool Woolrich jacket.

By the early 1900's, vacations were no longer limited to the middle class. Working-class people began to share in the benefits of regular time off work while enjoying nature and outdoor sports.

Organized and team sports came into their own, as well, and companies like Woolrich supplied the proper clothing. The U.S. Golf Association was formed in 1894 and the sport soared in popularity as new courses were built. In 1895 there were fifty clubs with golf courses; by 1900 there were 1,040. Basketball, tennis, baseball, and football all caught on with Americans who were beginning to have the leisure time needed to enjoy watching and partici-pating in these sports.

This 1925 Woolrich advertisement reflects the emerging interest in dressing right for a variety of sports ranging from golf and skiing to boating and fishing.

RICH'S SPORT BLOUSES

ALL young America and those who persist in staying young are sporting these colorful garments. The snappy, bright patterns can be seen on every high school playground, college campus, athletic field, on every street, on the golf links, on the tennis court, and they are ideal for boating, fishing, motoring; in fact, there are no sports that cannot be served to advantage by these good-looking, service-able blouses. They add a welcome touch of color in dress, and this style has defi-nitely established itself as one of the dominant features for *all* seasons of the year.

See attached price list.

Woolrich

Woolrich continued to expand steadily as recreational markets grew. New structures were added regularly to the mill operation: a two-story brick wool storage building in 1909, a picker room in 1912, a new store building in 1915, and a mill addition in 1917. When the U.S. entered World War I in 1917, Woolrich was commissioned to make blankets for the Army, much as it had done during the Civil War.

The United States had conquered its frontier, expanded from coast to coast, and weathered a bitter civil war. Business was expanding, fueled by new inventions and a growing population of immigrants. Wave after wave of change swept over the country: the Wright brothers' first successful flight in 1903, the development of radio in the mid-twenties, transcontinental telephone service and women's suffrage in 1920. The most profound change, it is easily argued, was brought on by the introduction

(top) Looms preparing wool fabric in the Woolrich weaving room. (above) Women converting wool fabric into finished goods in the sewing room at the Woolrich mill.

Two campers enjoy the newfound freedom the automobile provided at the Boiling Spring Camp Ground, Cleveland National Forest, California. This scene was photographed circa 1910.

of the mass-produced automobile. Henry Ford introduced the Model T in 1909, and by 1926 his assembly line in Detroit was turning out a Model T every ten seconds. In 1916, 1.5 million automobiles were sold in the United States, and by 1929 there were 23 million cars on the roads.

Woolrich

The automobile gave average Americans unprecedented freedom to explore the country, free of train schedules and even the cost and bother of staying in hotels. Automobile owners took to the growing network of roads to explore the American landscape, staying in auto-camps and roadside cabins, while fueling up at gas stations and eating at the new phenomenon of drive-in restaurants.

In the little settlement of Woolrich, the winds of change were being felt as well. Operations began to expand beyond the mill settlement. In 1919 a tipple was built in McElhattan, a few miles to the southeast. The next year the company opened a garment manufacturing unit in Avis, just six miles east of the mill. Further additions to the mill complex

▶ **1910**

Founding of Boy Scouts of America and Camp Fire Girls

Woolrich leather-faced mittens, shown here drying on stretchers, were a staple in the early years.

The Woolrich sock room in 1910.

1920
Women vote for the first time

On December 27, 1927, W. B. Rich placed a statement on the company bulletin board that summarized the Woolrich company's principles:

FAIR PLAY

Civilization is Team Work.

Good Team Work Simply Means Fair Play.

Fair Play for Everyone on the team.

The more men work together, the better they understand that Fair Play for each individual helps everybody.

In our organization we all know that success lies in the slogan—"Fair Play for Everyone."

included a box shed and a wool storage building in 1924, a new boiler house and stock in 1926, and a storage building in 1927.

In 1923 the Woolrich community enjoyed a curious footnote to history by being acclaimed the "automobile capital of the world." Seventy-one families in Woolrich owned seventy-six automobiles.

Mailbags full of wool from the mill are transported to the railroad siding in McElhattan by horse-drawn wagon. In winter, the wheels were replaced with sleigh runners.

Centennial Celebration

The Jazz Age of the 1920's brought prosperity and new freedom for the middle and upper classes. But all that changed abruptly on October 29, 1929, when the stock market crashed. Soon the United States was plunged into the Great Depression. Although the economic malaise was undoubtedly felt as Woolrich celebrated its centennial anniversary in 1930, the company remained sound and active, with plenty of reason to celebrate 100 years of success. The company roster listed 216 employees, many from the same families and many the children

Children join the centennial parade through the streets of Woolrich.

or grandchildren of people who had worked at the Woolrich mill in earlier years. The names of the various departments reflected the process of making wool: carding, picking and spinning; warping room; weave room; cutting department; sew room; finishing department; dye room; knitting room; packing and shipping department; and the Avis shirt plant. A sales force of nineteen, headed by J. B. Rich, covered much of the nation from Maine to Alaska, Florida to California.

So from July 25–27, 1930, Woolrich set aside three days to celebrate its 100 years as a successful business. A grand street parade was arranged complete with the Woolrich Band, floats from the mill and out of town, and decorated cars. Woolrich clowns entertained at the swimming pool where there were swimming races, a tug o' war, and a water ball game. Former Governor Gifford Pinchot delivered an address. "Races, comic contests, feats of strength" were held at the baseball field, followed by a spirited ball game between Lock Haven and Woolrich. Old-time fiddlers competed for the top prize. On Sunday, there were religious services, band and orchestral concerts, and Sunday school conducted at the Woolrich Community Church. You could buy a dinner or supper on Friday and Saturday for 75 and 50 cents, respectively. Sunday dinner was a dollar.

▶ **1923**

Henry Luce founds *Time* magazine

Clinton County's paper, *The Express,* heralded the event by noting the close ties between the company and the surrounding community: "In Woolrich, the chief concern is the manufacture of a product in such a way that all those who

The Woolrich Woolen Mills, decorated with patriotic bunting, announces the centennial.

join in the industrial process shall be rewarded with prosperity and the opportunity to live a pleasant life in attractive surroundings and under wholesome conditions."

In 1930 the Woolrich Woolen Mills, now incorporated, boasted an assortment of handsome brick buildings housing the full wool-making process. Raw fleece was delivered in bales at one end of the complex, and finished wool products came out the other end, ready for shipment throughout the country.

An impressive community supported the mill and its workers. In addition to the church and general store, there was a new brick schoolhouse, a community swimming pool, a baseball park and company-sponsored baseball team, a post office, a community building, and a twenty-acre park.

Cover of the 1927 Woolrich catalog.

Woolrich sponsored a community baseball team that played at the company-owned ballpark.

54

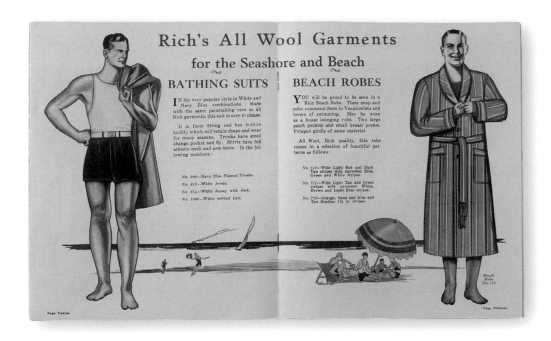

Rich's All Wool Garments

for the Seashore and Beach

BATHING SUITS

IN the very popular style in White and Navy Blue combinations. Made with the same painstaking care as all Rich garments, this suit is sure to please.

It is form fitting and has built-in quality which will retain shape and wear for many seasons. Trunks have small change pocket and fly. Shirts have full athletic neck and arm holes. In the following numbers:

No. 200—Navy Blue Flannel Trunks.
No. 212—White Jersey.
No. 214—White Jersey with Jock.
No. 1000—White webbed Belt.

BEACH ROBES

YOU will be proud to be seen in a Rich Beach Robe. Their snap and color commend them to Vacationists and lovers of swimming. May be worn as a house lounging robe. Two large patch pockets and small breast pocket. Fringed girdle of same material.

All Wool, Rich quality, this robe comes in a selection of beautiful patterns as follows:

No. 710—Wide Light Red and Dark Tan stripes with narrower Blue, Green and White stripes.

No. 711—Wide Light Tan and Green stripes with narrower White, Brown and Light Blue stripes.

No. 715—Orange, Sand and Blue and Tan Heather 1¼ in. stripes.

Beach Robe No. 710

The 1930 catalog provided to Woolrich dealers included a wide assortment of woolen goods, ranging from Misses' Ski Coats and Ski Trousers to wool Angler's Shirts, Fishing Trousers, and Norfolk Sport Coat. There was an all-wool Union Suit called "Old Reliable" and men's wool bathing outfit that included tank top, shorts, and a rustproof belt. At the heart of the catalog were the wool flannel

▶ **1930–31**

Automobile robes and steamer rugs are focal items for Woolrich, and all-wool angler's jackets are introduced

shirts that had made the company famous, along with several varieties of hunting coats and the famous Woolrich Work Vest (or Railroad Vest, as it is now known). Women could select various colors of the Woolrich Novelty Sport Suit, a brightly striped winter jacket with matching trousers. There were several wool blankets and Automobile Robes, as well as playsuits

(left) "Norwegian-Style Ski, Skating and Hiking garments" are featured in the 1930 catalog. Colors included crimson red, Nile green, royal blue, and navy blue.

237 Cap	234 Cap	236 Cap		233 Cap
877 Suit	874 Suit	876 Suit		873 Suit
437 Mittens	434 Mittens	436 Mittens		433 Mittens

Woolrich Children's Play Suits

A comfortable, all wool combination Play Suit. Cap and mittens to match. Made of 22 oz. weather-proof cloth. Talon Fastener on front and legs. Button flap drop seat. The Talon Fastener, the never failing device, is far superior to the worsted bottoms and are much easier to put on and take off. A worsted bottom will not give the wear required of a child's play suit and will soon wear off and look shabby. The Talon Fastener will always keep its shape. These garments, from every standpoint, are the best and most practical child's play suit on the market. Ages: 2 to 12.

870—Maroon and Black Broken Bar.
871—Plain Maroon.
872—Plain Chocolate Brown.
873—Plain Red.
874—Fawn Color.
876—Plain Royal Blue.
877—Plain Nile Green.
878—Blue and Black Broken Bar.
879—Green and Black Broken Bar.

Woolrich Children's Aviation Caps

Match above suits, are duvetyn lined and of the same material as the Play Suits. These are the addition necessary to make the suits perfection. Sizes: 6¼ to 7¼.

230—To match 870 Suit.
231—To match 871 Suit.
232—To match 872 Suit.
233—To match 873 Suit.
234—To match 874 Suit.
236—To match 876 Suit.
237—To match 877 Suit.
238—To match 878 Suit.
239—To match 879 Suit.

Woolrich Children's Play Mittens

Made of same cloth as Play Suits to match. Knitted wrist, snappy tailored and lined. Three sizes to one dozen box.

430—To match 870 Play Suit.
431—To match 871 Play Suit.
432—To match 872 Play Suit.
433—To match 873 Play Suit.
434—To match 874 Play Suit.
436—To match 876 Play Suit.
437—To match 877 Play Suit.
438—To match 878 Play Suit.
439—To match 879 Play Suit.

Children's Play Suits in brightly colored wool are offered in the 1930's.

and short jackets ("blouses" in the terminology of the day) for children, and golf knickers and blouses for men. An elegant all-wool bathrobe came in several colors. Wool socks were offered in a full range of styles.

In an address at the Woolrich centennial celebration on July 25, 1930, (as reported in the *Lock Haven Express*), M. B. Rich pointed out that the current population of Woolrich stood at 85 families that possessed 36 pianos, 31 victrolas, and 70 other musical instruments, along with 56 radios. The paper noted that "the census now places 476 people, seven hogs, five cows, 23 dogs, and 702 chickens."

For the outdoor and sport enthusiast, wool was the fabric of choice, and Woolrich had a century's worth of experience producing the finest wool products.

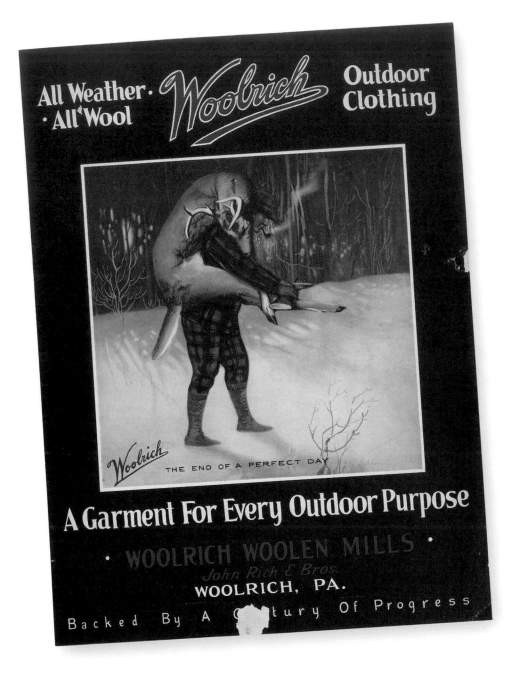

Challenging Times

Woolrich survived the Depression intact. During the worst years, the company used plant employees to build more company houses, rather than lay off workers.

By 1939, the population of Woolrich consisted of 435 people, and the mill was producing socks, gloves, underwear, jackets, shirts, and other outdoor garments, supplying, as *The Express* put it, "nearly every corner of the nation where chilly Winters create a need for woolen warmth." Woolrich recorded some $1.5 million in sales for the year.

In 1939 Admiral Richard E. Byrd, who had become a national hero after two previous expeditions to Antarctica, launched his third expedition. Byrd joined forces with the U.S. government on this expedition with the ambitious goal of surveying much of the little explored continent between two outposts that were 2,200 miles apart by sea. The Woolrich Woolen Mills

Grit, a national newspaper published in Williamsport, Pennsylvania, carried the story of Woolrich's work making garments for Admiral Byrd's third expedition to Antarctica.

were chosen to provide woolen clothing to help the 125-man expeditionary crew survive temperatures that would reach 60 degrees below zero.

Woolrich geared up for the expedition to "Little America" in the Antarctic and went into production of 1,296 all-wool garments that included medium and heavy wool shirts, reinforced ski pants, special red-and-black hunting breeches, 32-ounce wool pants, and special virgin wool hunting coats. The Byrd expedition crew returned to the States in early 1941 after successfully exploring and surveying vast areas of the Antarctic continent.

▶ **1941**

The Japanese attack Pearl Harbor

As Byrd was launching his expedition to the southernmost continent, the drumbeat of war was sounding across Europe. In September of 1939 Hitler invaded Poland, and Britain and France declared war on Germany. World War II had begun. After trying to maintain neutrality for two years, the United States was drawn into the war after the surprise attack on Pearl Harbor on December 7, 1941.

Once again, Woolrich geared up its woolen mill to support the war effort—much as it had done during the Civil War and World War I—by making blankets and uniforms for the armed services.

This nearly life-size die-cut was found in the basement of the C. F. Biddle clothing store in Canton, Pennsylvania. The store had been closed for many years. This was found in mint condition, with original packing box dated 1947.

Woolrich

Pearce Woolen Mill

The Pearce Manufacturing Company was established in 1805 at Harmony, Pennsylvania, by the Harmonite Society. The company manufactured Pearce wool blankets at that site until it moved to Greenville, Pennsylvania, in 1886. Destroyed by fire in 1904, the plant moved to Latrobe.

In 1928 Woolrich bought the Pearce Manufacturing Company, and the operation continued in Latrobe under the management of the Pearce family. In 1959 the Latrobe mill was closed, and the Pearce line of blankets and woolens was incorporated into operations at the mill in Woolrich.

One of the legacies of the Pearce operation was that it was the exclusive U.S. distributor of the famous Hudson's Bay Point Blankets that had been imported from England by the Hudson's Bay Company since 1779. In the late 1700's, wool blankets were so important to comfort and survival that they were used as a form of currency in trading between trappers and Native Americans. Beaver pelts were exchanged for blankets through the Hudson's Bay Company and its outposts throughout Northern Canada. Higher-quality blankets (usually larger) were assigned more points, and the point designation was woven as short stripes (or points) on the edge of the blanket. Although the exchange rate varied, points were often the measure of the number of beaver pelts the blankets would bring in exchange with the Native American trappers.

When Woolrich acquired the Pearce Manufacturing Company, it also acquired the official license to distribute the blankets in the United States, a distinction it proudly maintains today. Modern bed sizes dictate the point sizes today: a 4-point blanket fits a full-size bed, a 6-point a queen, and an 8-point a king.

The Baby Boom

When World War II ended, American servicemen streamed home to start families, build houses, and join an ever-expanding consumer society. The baby boom was born. During the 1950's, the new middle class spread out into the fast-growing suburbs. "Ozzie and Harriet" and "Leave It to Beaver" were on television, and TV sets were appearing in more and more homes. In 1954, a young man named Elvis Presley walked into Sun Records in Memphis and changed music forever.

Vacations were now an accepted reality for all Americans, rich and poor. Traveling by car received an enormous boost with the passage of the Interstate Highway Act in 1956. It would result in 42,000 miles of new high-speed highways.

1952–53 Woolrich catalog.

Expanding and Modernizing

In 1953, Roswell Brayton, Sr. was offered a job as a textile engineer with the Woolrich Company by his father-in-law, Robert F. Rich. Brayton had been employed in Fall River, Massachusetts. The once booming textile industry in Fall River was coming to an end, and Brayton looked forward to putting his experience to work at Woolrich where business was still brisk.

He arrived in September 1953, with his wife, Catherine, and three children—five-year-old Anne, seven-year-old Charlotte, and two-year-old Roswell Jr. ("Rozzie"). The company was being managed by E. C. Tobias, under the leadership of Robert F. Rich who had recently retired from Congress.

Robert Fleming Rich

When M. B. Rich died in 1930, his son Robert Fleming Rich became general manager and served in that capacity until 1959, when he became president. He gave up the presidency in 1964 to become chairman of the board and continued daily participation in the company until 1966, when he became honorary chairman of the board. In all, Robert F. Rich served the company for over seventy years—a period that began in 1896 when he worked during summer vacations at the plant until his retirement as full-time chairman of the board.

In addition to his work with the company, he served in Congress for eighteen years from 1931 to 1951, with the exception of two years, 1943–45. Rich was a staunch Republican of the old school who became famous in Congress for the phrase, "Where are we going to get the money?" Like so many of his family members, he was active in local church, educational, and philanthropic activities.

After his death in 1968 at the age of 84, Robert F. Rich's passing and his many years of service were recognized by the House of Representatives. Congressman Gerald R. Ford, then minority leader of the House and later, of course, president of the United States, was among those who spoke to honor him: "He was a man of deep conviction and dedicated to principle," Ford said. "He was also one of the most lovable, one of the kindest, one of the most generous Members of this body. He was a delight to be with. He was a worker of untiring energy. He left an indelible mark in the House of Representatives."

When Brayton arrived, he recalls, there were about fifty mill-owned houses renting from $10 to $15 a month. Some of the larger houses rented to boarders. Water from Chatham Run was still diverted to a millpond, and the water released from the pond drove a turbine that provided power as well as water for scouring and dyeing the fabric. Most of the community services and utilities—including water, electric, garbage, fire protection, and the like—were still provided by Woolrich to village residents.

As both the village and the woolen company expanded, Woolrich began to divest itself of the village services. In the sixties, for example, Brayton remembers the vice president of the power company, Pennsylvania Power and Light Company, approaching Woolrich about buying the electrical service to the community. "My company is in the electric business, and you're in the woolen business. Don't you think you'd be better off selling your electric system and you concentrate on the woolen business?" The logic seemed unassailable to Woolrich and a deal was struck. Similarly, Woolrich started a television service for residents and, once it was established, sold it to a local company.

(right) The 1954 catalog featured "Mountain Made Woolens" for hunters.

For many years, the company collected weekly trash and charged residents $5 per month. As the community grew, that operation was turned over to a company that had the proper trash trucks. Fire service to the Woolrich buildings was provided with an in-house fire crew and a company fire engine. As the village expanded, it set up its own volunteer fire crew and Woolrich turned the fire engine over to the village. Lawrence Schlesinger, Woolrich's head of internal fire safety and head electrician, also served as chief of the village voluntary fire department.

▶ **1950**
The Korean War begins

By 1960, the community had outgrown its small post office in the company store. The federal government sought bids for expansion, and

Woolrich

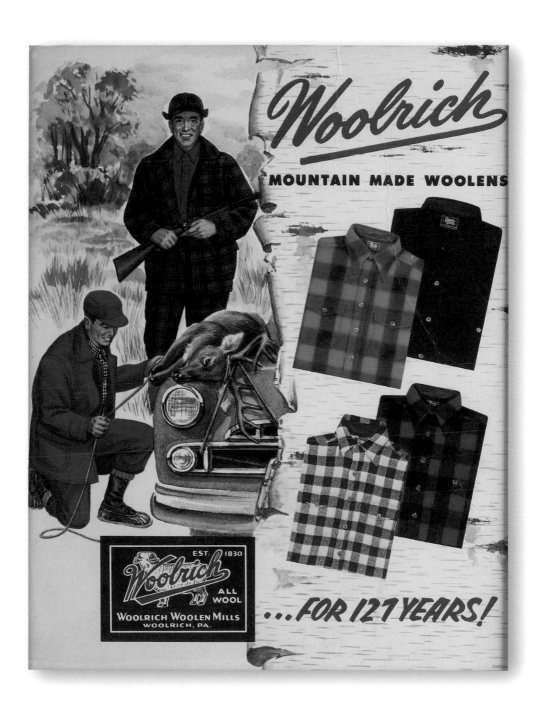

Woolrich submitted a plan to build the new post office on its land. The government accepted and the new post office was built and leased back to the government. Shortly after, Woolrich sold the building and land at cost to the Woolrich Community Church, providing the church with a steady income.

One of the first things Brayton set about doing when he arrived was to upgrade the equipment in the mill, which had seen many years of service but was growing out of date. He purchased some used machinery from a mill near Hartford, Connecticut, that had gone out of business; included were machines for burling and mending, perching, and inspecting.

Woolrich offerings in the 1950's and early 1960's feature blankets and basic outdoor wear, including socks, mittens, and wool outfits for hunting, skiing, and other outdoor sports.

Brayton explains:

"A burling and mending machine is composed of a steel framework supporting a slanted glass wider than the cloth. The front surface is a frosted glass with lights underneath. The operator has a chair with castors so she can move back and forth as she burls the cloth. The burler removes noticeable defects in the cloth such as slubs and double ends. 'Mending' is the term for replacing a missing or wrong end of yarn by sewing in the correct yarn.

A worker adjusts a spinning frame in the Woolrich mill.

"The way it was done at Woolrich previous to the new machines was for the operator to pull the cloth over a freely moving roll and rub her hands back and forth over the surface to feel for any defects. With the new machine, the cloth traveled over a lighted glass, and defects could be seen." He says that the machines cut the burling time in half and required much less physical energy.

Fulling—compacting the cloth in both length and width—is the next operation in the wool making process. A roll of cloth, for example, that starts out 74 inches wide and averages 28 ounces per yard comes out of the fulling machine 60 inches wide and averages 32 ounces per yard. The new fulling machines allowed an operator to do twice as much wool in a week. Brayton also oversaw upgrades in Woolrich looms and the finishing department where modern napping machines—used to create a soft finish on the surface of the wool—

▶ **1963**

President John F. Kennedy is assassinated

Roswell Brayton, Sr.

could nap three times faster than the old ones.

New looms were added—first the much faster Dornier looms from Germany, followed by even faster Sulzer looms from Switzerland. A new building was built for the looms, and the finishing department was centralized next to the weaving department. Further improvements continued to be made over the 1960's and 1970's, including automatic humidification and the methods for moving wool from the picker house to the card room. When the yarn manufacturing capacity doubled, Brayton received approval to build a new weaving and warping building. A carbonizing range was installed to remove all cellulose matter in the fabric, including leaf fibers, seeds, and cotton.

In 1968 Robert F. Rich died, and Roswell Brayton, Sr. was chosen as the new president of the company.

(right) In 1960, the Woolrich line of clothing reflects an increased interest in style.

▶ **1964**
Martin Luther King, Jr. receives the Nobel Prize for Peace

Changing Times

Woolrich had introduced men's and women's plaid "TV Jackets" in the early 1950's just as America was discovering the first wave of the electronic media revolution. But changes in American society were coming faster and faster. For one thing, the textile industry in America was no longer dependent solely on natural fibers like cotton, flax, silk, and wool—fabrics that had been around for thousands of years. Man-made fibers were invented and began to be used for apparel. Rayon was the first man-made fiber, introduced in 1910. Nylon

Pace-setting NEW sports fashions by . . .

Woolrich

WOOLRICH WOOLEN MILLS
WOOLRICH, PENNSYLVANIA

EST. 1830
Woolrich
ALL WOOL
WOOLRICH WOOLEN MILLS
WOOLRICH, PA.

130 YEARS OF QUALITY
OUTDOOR WOOLENS

appeared in 1939, followed by acrylic in 1950, polyester in 1953, spandex in 1959, and polypropylene in 1961.

Although wool hunting coats, wool blankets, and rugged wool shirts continued to be in demand and kept the looms running at the Woolrich mills, the company adapted to the changing times. Lighter and more specialized clothing was being demanded by outdoor-oriented consumers.

One of the most profound changes in consumer tastes started in the late 1960's with the "back to the earth" movement. Young people, many of whom had converged on San Francisco in 1967 for the "Summer of Love" and "be-ins" in Golden Gate Park, became intensely interested in raising their own natural food, hiking, backpacking, and camping. It wasn't long before this youth movement had spread to the older generation, as well. Colin Fletcher's *The Complete Walker* was published in 1968 and went on to sell nearly half a million copies in its various editions.

The new sensibilities were welcome news at the little village of Woolrich. After all, folks there had been supplying the outdoor market for nearly 140 years. But adaptation was the key. Rather than relying exclusively on its past, Woolrich actively pursued the new markets.

1969–70 Woolrich catalog.

Woolrich developed woolens geared to the collegiate crowd, as seen in these 1962 covers.

New sewing centers were created. Eventually there would be nine plants sewing Woolrich garments: five in Pennsylvania, two in Colorado, and one each in Nebraska and the state of Washington.

Backpacking brought with it a need for warm clothing that was lightweight. Goose and duck down fill was just the thing. Down vests and jackets became de rigueur on the backpacking trail, and soon they were being worn nearly everywhere. William Ferry, the company's vice president of merchandising at the time, observed: "We design our clothing for a particular use, but the great percentage of those garments are bought to be worn in the shopping centers and football stadiums of America. And it makes sense. When you think of the principles of such concepts as layered clothing, they are no less valid for the guy who has just emptied his flask at the last quarter of the Penn State game than they are for a hunter."

The Woolrich Chamois Shirt.

The Woolrich Chamois Shirt—one of the most popular products in

▶ **1969**
Neil Armstrong is the first man to walk on the moon

the history of the company—was introduced in 1969. This brushed cotton shirt exemplified the new interest in performance fabrics that were light, rugged, and useful for weekend wear as well as strenuous outdoor activities.

In 1972 Woolrich introduced the original Arctic Parka, the quintessential down parka designed to handle the most extreme temperatures. It was originally designed for workers constructing the Alaskan pipeline, where the average winter low is minus twenty-five degrees Farenheit. The Arctic Parka became very popular among recreational users braving cold temperatures, and over the years it has gained popularity throughout the world, particularly in Italy where it remains a smash hit among young people.

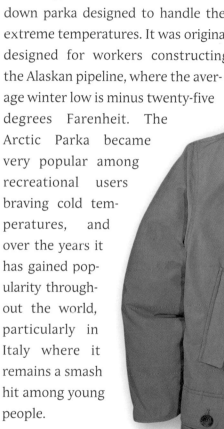

The Woolrich Arctic Parka.

The original wool-lined Woolrich Mountain Parka was introduced in 1978 and has gone on to become a signature garment for the company. As a basic layering jacket for a variety of outdoor activities, it set the pace for hikers and campers, as well as suburbanites. In 1973 Woolrich acquired the Down Products Corporation, which had plants in Colorado and Washington. By 1980 only about 30 percent of the total clothing line contained wool. The other garments were made from cotton, poplin, and synthetic fibers. New, lighter fabrics meant that Woolrich could also now offer a spring line of garments. Previous sales had concentrated, of necessity, on the fall and winter months.

In the late 1970's, the Woolrich Mountain Parka was a huge success with young people who were taking to the outdoors in increased numbers.

The product line during the 1970's reflected not only the renewed interest in the outdoors, but styles that owed more to the growing world of media-inspired fashion. Items like the "Mad Mod Vest" in tartan wool and "Hip Fringed Vest" debuted, and perhaps sent a shiver of regret through some old-time Woolrich customers for whom the "Pennsylvania Tuxedo" was fashion enough.

At a time when most of the early woolen mills in the United States had disappeared, Woolrich business was booming. In the nearly two decades between 1961 and 1979, Woolrich sales multiplied fifteen-fold. In 1980, Brayton observed, "There's only been one year since I came here in 1953 that I saw sales curtailed drastically. That was in 1957. We had a recession that hit the textile industry very, very hard."

February 17, 2005
Woolrich
One Mill Street
Woolrich, PA 17779

Dear Woolrichers:

I owe you thanks for a real bargain. One of your recent catalogs suggested, "Own a Piece of History." It reminded me that I already do—but not the Railroad Vest you were describing, but a 44-year-old red Woolrich jacket.

In 1961, my employer, Eastman Kodak Company, sent me to Alaska to make a travel movie, from Ketchikan to Point Barrow. Looking for something that would provide some warmth while adding a spot of color, I purchased a red Woolrich jacket in Rochester, New York, for $10.00.

My partner and I took still pictures of each other to use in promoting the movie, which we showed under the sponsorship of local newspapers in major auditoriums all over the country, from the Seattle Opera House to Hartford, CT.

Well, I've worn it and worn it and worn it. My wife had to re-sew the buttonholes, but other than that, it's as good as ever. Thanks for the bargain.

Sincerely,

Jack M. Streb

Jack Streb pictured in 2005 in his 44-year-old Woolrich jacket.

In 1961 Jack Streb wears his new Woolrich jacket as he inspects a Russian Orthodox graveyard just north of Anchorage, Alaska.

Woolrich at 150

When 1980 arrived it was time for another celebration. The company had reached the milestone of 150 years in business, nearly all of it headquartered at the same small plant and community in rural Pennsylvania. It was a rare occurrence in the business world and an even rarer one in the volatile wool and garment industry. Of the hundreds of woolen mills that once dotted the country, only a handful survived.

The demand for functional outdoor clothing was still strong, and the recent energy crisis had Americans lowering their thermostats and reaching for a wool shirt or sweater. The "preppy" trend was also underway, and Woolrich's khaki sales suddenly jumped 30 percent.

Woolrich Appreciation Week was scheduled for mid-June 1980. A banner spanned Main Street in nearby Lock Haven announcing "Woolrich, Inc., 150 Years of Doing It Right." There were plant tours, along with sheep-shearing, wool-spinning, and weaving demonstrations. Woolrich also used the occasion to induct four famous American outdoorsmen into the Woolrich Outdoor Hall of Fame. The inductees included Lowell Thomas, a well-known world traveler and newscaster; Leon Gorman, president of L. L. Bean; James Whittaker, the first American to reach the peak of Mount Everest; and Laurence Gould, noted geologist, author, and polar explorer.

▶ **1981**
The first space shuttle, Columbia, is launched

Business was booming. Woolrich employed some 1,900 workers in plants located in Pennsylvania; Denver and Broomfield, Colorado; Seattle, Washington; and Alliance, Nebraska. In its home base of Clinton County and neighboring Lycoming County, Woolrich had five facilities: trousers and knickers were made in Jersey Shore; shirts in Avis; jackets in Howard and Blanchard; and wool

fabric at the mill in Woolrich. The Woolrich plant employed 900 workers. All told, Woolrich produced four million garments each year.

The 1980 Woolrich product catalog is testament to the fact that the world of style had come Woolrich's way. Here were the kind of rugged outdoor garments Woolrich had always been known for, but now in a full blossoming of fabrics, designs, and functions. "Fashion is fine," the catalog proclaimed, "provided it is fashion that people can use and enjoy for years." There were the traditional wool shirts and hunting coats, plus down vests, Arctic Parkas, chamois shirts, wool-lined mountain parkas, Ragg sweaters, cross-country and downhill ski outfits in modern new fibers, and folks wrapped up in cozy wool blankets.

(previous page and above) This 1980 catalog reflects an interest by both younger and older Americans in fashions that had practical applications in the outdoors.

Woolrich goods were on sale throughout the United States, including in the many backpacking and specialty shops that had cropped up in recent years to cater to skiers, backpackers, hunters, and serious mountain climbers.

In the early 1980's, Woolrich began the process of computerizing some of its machinery. New

Woolrich

materials like Gore-Tex®, Thinsulate®, and Cordura® were used to enhance the perform-ance of wool. In 1986 its line of hunting goods included the new CamWOOLflage®, all-wool cam-ouflage. Jackets constructed out of the new material were mar-ried with Gore-Tex® to produce warm, waterproof, and breath-able gear. Woolrich reached out internationally as well, with business in Canada, Italy, and Japan.

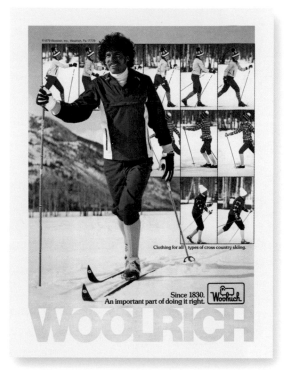

Roswell Brayton, Sr. retired as president in December 1985 and S. Wade Judy, who had been senior vice president of finance, was named president and CEO of the corporation. Judy remained president until 1993 and helped steer the company through its early phases of transition from being a manufacturing company to becoming a marketing company. In 1993 H. Varnell Moore joined the company as president and CEO. He served in those roles until 1996 and was instrumental in accelerating the pace of the company's sourcing of products on a worldwide basis. Roswell Brayton, Sr. remained as chairman of the board until March 31, 1996.

By 1988 Woolrich was making 7.8 million garments in ten plants and distributing them through three shipping locations in Nebraska, Jersey Shore, and Woolrich. The woolen mill was still completely integrated: that is, cleaned

Woolrich for Women

Woolrich's primary customers had always been men, although the company did pioneer women's outdoor clothing as early as 1915 when Woolrich offered double-front Mackinaw coats and wool hose for ladies. But it wasn't until the early 1980's that the company began to design and market a whole line of clothing directed specifically to women. Today, women's clothing is one of the most important components of the Woolrich line.

FALL 1989 FOR WOMEN

bales arrived at the plant and all operations including dyeing, spinning, weaving, and finishing were done in the mill. The fabric was then ready to be cut into apparel or blankets or used for furniture or wall panels. The mill processed some 5.2 million pounds of wool per year, most of it from American sheep growers.

Although Woolrich always prided itself on enduring designs that changed little over time, the fashions of the new consumer-oriented industry did take their toll. The demand for puffy down garments, for example, dropped dramatically. Eventually, Woolrich would close all of its down-filled apparel plants, with the exception of the Jersey Shore plant, which still produces down-filled Arctic Parkas.

Increasingly, other fabrics and garments were being produced overseas, particularly in the Far East, at much lower costs. The global economy was underway and U.S. barriers to cheaper overseas fabrics were being eliminated. The 1990's proved to be a decade of drastic change for the apparel industry, and Woolrich could not escape the flood of new merchandise.

Woolrich

Woolrich Today

Roswell Brayton, Jr. became president of Woolrich in 1996, and assumed the CEO position a year later. He was in a unique position. A sixth-generation of the Rich family, he had literally grown up in and around the Woolrich factory. One of his favorite activities as a young boy was baseball, and he played for the Woolrich Little League team where he developed a love for the game. After schooling at the Milton Academy and Harvard University, Roz, as he was known, was drafted by the Boston Red Sox and spent the next four years playing professional baseball. With his big league dreams behind him, Roz returned to the Woolrich business in 1978, first serving as a sales representative for Kentucky and part of Indiana before returning to the main office in Woolrich.

"In the last ten years," Brayton notes, "we've become a lifestyle company, with a whole range of goods related to the outdoors." Brayton admits that one of the toughest times for Woolrich was the 1990's, as the business adapted once again to changes in the business climate. "But the last four years have been very good and have shown that we're on the right track again." Brayton gives much of the credit for growth to the company's long-term planning. "And we reinvest most of our earnings back into the company," he adds.

Rick Insley, senior vice-president for international licensing and retail, has been at the forefront of the company's change in direction to meet the demands of the modern business world. "We are truly a global brand now," Insley says. Woolrich's entry into the world market started some two decades

▶ **1980's**
Woolrich launches international business in Canada, Italy, and Japan

ago with a licensing agreement with WP Lavori, an Italian company. Lavori set up Woolrich products in stores throughout Italy. "They did such a good job," Insley says, "that five years ago they were given the rights to distribute

The Woolrich brand received a major boost in Europe with the recent opening of stores in Paris, France (above) and Italy.

Woolrich products throughout Europe and Russia, under the direction of Dennis Marxen, vice president of international and home licensing." Three new stores selling Woolrich exclusively have opened recently in Cortina and Courmayeur, Italy, and in Paris, France. A licensing agreement was just signed for Australia, and plans call for bringing Woolrich to China in the near future.

In Japan, Woolrich has worked for some twenty years with Tomen Corporation, a master licensee that arranges sublicenses with various manufacturers for apparel, shoes, gloves, hats, belts, handbags, and children's clothing. Woolrich is also represented by Xebio, Japan's premier chain of sporting goods stores. "The history of the Woolrich brand is extremely important in Europe and Japan," Insley adds.

Recently Woolrich launched a home products line in Lexington, North Carolina. The products—

(top right) The Paris store interior has one wall devoted to a map of the Woolrich, Pennsylvania, area. (below right) The interior of the new store in Cortina, Italy, has a look familiar to Woolrich shoppers anywhere.

Woolrich

including lighting, rugs, dishes, placemats, bed covers, and wallpaper—are sold in furniture stores throughout the country.

Maintaining a strong brand means that Woolrich must devote more of its resources to designing and merchandising the apparel it sells. That begins in Woolrich with a core of a dozen designers, merchandisers, and support people who put together each year's line of clothing. Heading that effort is Lederle Eberhardt, vice president of design and merchandising.

When Eberhardt started with the company a decade ago, she was the only merchandiser for women and she had one counterpart in the men's department. "Back then," she says, "80 percent of the line was repeated each

Lederle Eberhardt (left) and some members of her design team review fabrics for upcoming product lines.

NATURAL. AUTHENTIC. WOOLRICH.

EST. 1830
WOOLRICH
The Original Outdoor Clothing Company

This 2005 Woolrich ad is indicative of the new focus on women's designs.

year and 20 percent was new. Now the figures are reversed. There is much more emphasis on innovation and unique styling."

As the women's end of the business has grown to become such a large part of Woolrich sales, more effort goes into designing outfits for women with integrated color, texture, and design. "We've done a lot to make the women's line more feminine," Eberhardt adds.

In addition to the design and merchandising team in Woolrich, Pennsylvania, the company maintains an office in New York City where two of the designers live. "This helps us keep our pulse on the New York market," she says. "The great thing about our whole design department, though, is that they all live the outdoors lifestyle. They know what Woolrich is all about."

Once products are designed, they are now sourced throughout the world. That responsibility falls under the management of Charles Aides, senior vice president for apparel, manufacturing, and sourcing. "Fabrics come from all over the planet," Aides says, "although our two largest suppliers are China and India." The movement to offshore production began in the early 1990's, Aides says, and started with fabrics made in the U.S. but sewn overseas. The realities of modern trade agreements, however, have shifted the entire production of goods overseas in the last several years.

Offshore sourcing puts even greater emphasis on the design and merchandising group in Woolrich. Highly detailed specifications are sent to suppliers, prototypes are created, and a great deal of attention is paid to the final fit and finish of the garments.

One trend supporting U.S. production, however, is government contracts. Woolrich recently signed a five-year agreement to produce a combination of products for the military. Aides notes that Woolrich also works with countries in trade zones set up by the U.S. government to promote peaceful relations.

The Woolrich brand is expanding dramatically in the United States, as well. Domestic licensing now includes a variety of products including gloves, scarves, socks, hats, slippers, watches, belts, wallets, and children's wear. In 2006 the company hopes to add luggage. Jerry Rinder, vice president for sales and domestic licensing, is excited by the prospects for Woolrich. "Woolrich stands on its own merit," he says. "We are simply bringing the brand back to its rightful place in the apparel industry."

▶ 1990–94
Woolrich begins using six-color looms, automated cutting systems, computer-controlled workstations, and other new technologies.

A Familiar Message

In 2000 Woolrich established a Web site and began sending catalogs directly to consumers. Tim Joseph was brought in to launch the catalog and now directs the marketing and advertising department. He says the company is finding new ways to deliver an old message.

"We're actively exploring new channels of communication with our customers and dealers," he says, "but the message hasn't changed much in nearly two centuries: We make high-quality products at a good value for people who enjoy the outdoor lifestyle."

Rinder says the sales force, which is now selling the complete line of Woolrich goods, is enthusiastically embracing the new strategy. "The brand is everything," he says. "But with that comes a major responsibility. This brand has survived for one hundred and seventy-five years. Now it is our job to see that it survives another one hundred and seventy-five years."

Rinder believes the key to adding new products to the Woolrich line is maintaining excellent quality at a great value. "That's what Woolrich has always stood for," he says.

Woolrich built a new facility to house its marketing department directly across from the mill. The site was once occupied by M. B. Rich's home, which was preserved and moved up the hill.

Even the woolen mill is experiencing a bit of a renaissance under the new lifestyle-oriented business plan. Rick Osborne, vice president of the woolen mill, joined Woolrich in 1966. He has seen his share of change, but adds, "The principles of wool manufacturing have not changed much in the last one hundred years, although the weaving machines are much faster."

What has changed is the marketing of those wool products. With apparel manufacturing shifting dramatically to offshore sources, the Woolrich mill has focused on new, diverse markets. These now include small, high-quality specialty apparel manufacturers; uniform fabrics for groups like the Civil War re-enactors; wool blankets for Woolrich consumers and other civilian and government sources; upholstery; soft-sided luggage; and fabrics for high-end braided rugs. "We specialize in the niche markets now," Osborne says.

Another key player in making the transition to the new age of marketing and distribution is Bruce Heggenstaller, vice president of operations. Heggenstaller joined the company thirty-five years ago and has been instrumental in helping Woolrich emerge as a lifestyle company. "We've become a customer-centric company," he notes. "We determine what the customer wants and then find the best way to make it."

Heggenstaller has headed the creation of two new ways for Woolrich to sell its products directly to consumers—a direct-mail catalog and an Internet

Chatham Run still bubbles brightly through the village of Woolrich.

Woolrich

Web site. Both were launched in 2000. "Direct mail and the Web are important to the company," he explains, "because of the consolidation of distribution channels. When retail outlets were at their peak, we sold our goods through thousands of smaller retailers. Today buying habits have changed, and there are significantly fewer retailers available."

Direct-mail catalogs and the Web site also help Woolrich educate consumers about the brand, which in turn drives consumers to the retail stores. Woolrich maintains fourteen outlet stores for its goods, including the flagship store in the village of Woolrich.

Woolrich has always maintained a direct tie to the water that flows from the mountains down Chatham Run. It was the water, after all, that attracted John Rich II to this site in the first place. Water was necessary, at first, for power and has been in continuous demand for the wool-making operation. Now water is taking a new role in the Woolrich operations. Spring water from the 4,000-acre watershed owned by Woolrich above the town is now being bottled on site and marketed to the public. Initial plans call for selling Woolrich Spring Water to markets within four and one-half hours of the village, including major metropolitan centers in the mid-Atlantic region. Heggenstaller, who directs the project, says it is a logical extension of the Woolrich brand that fits perfectly into the Woolrich lifestyle. The 4,000-acre preserve, incidentally, remains open to the public for hiking, snowshoeing, and hunting.

The forest preserve is also home to another new project—Brayton Lodge. Situated at 1,722 feet elevation on the side of the mountain, the lodge has views as far as twenty-two miles away. The 7,000-square-foot structure with 1,800 feet of decking—built with Pennsylvania logs and stones from the Woolrich property—will serve as a showcase for Woolrich products to major customers and clients. It will give Woolrich a chance to show not only the goods manufactured in the historic mill, but the full range of licensed goods including furniture, lamps, rugs, wall artwork, and other items for the home that relate to the outdoor lifestyle.

The new Brayton Lodge is situated in the mountains above the village of Woolrich and serves as a showcase for the many Woolrich lifestyle products.

In the end, much of Woolrich's ability to succeed for 175 years, while so many others have failed, comes down to people. That's the view of Roger Sheets, vice president of human resources. In his years at Woolrich he has seen a great deal of change. Where there were once more than a dozen domestic production plants, there are now three. But employment is growing in areas like customer service, production planning, sourcing, and marketing.

Sheets says that Woolrich employees have been with the company an average of seventeen years. "People here are pretty proud of the Woolrich brand and who we are as a company," Sheets says. "Inevitably, they say they like working here because of the people they've worked with and the product they've worked on."

"We value longevity here," Sheets adds, pointing out that the company emphasizes training and development at all levels.

Woolrich

$\mathcal{T}$he village of Woolrich remains a quaint and quiet place—perhaps an unlikely site for one of America's most enduring businesses. The mill here still produces the wool for jackets, pants, and blankets that have become icons of the outdoor lifestyle. Bales of raw wool still come in one end of the mill and,

after a good deal of work, exit as warm fabric that is as functional today as it was in the middle of the nineteenth century.

The company, however, has changed dramatically. It now presides over a worldwide business. Woolrich designers create styles that are sourced wherever they can be produced best: in some cases, across the street at the mill; in many other cases, halfway around the globe. And Woolrich has expanded its core products to include a whole lifestyle dedicated to the enjoyment of the outside world.

Woolrich has endured as a business because it has had a remarkably stable line of ownership, because its workers have been dedicated and loyal and fairly treated, and because it has focused on doing what it does well while continually adapting to the needs of its customers. With a bit of luck, the words of Ralph Waldo Emerson will still ring true for many generations to come:

> *If a man can write a better book, preach a better sermon, or make a better mousetrap than his neighbor, though he build his house in the woods, the world will make a beaten path to his door.*

Selected Bibliography

Aron, Cindy S. *Working at Play: A History of Vacations in the United States.* New York: Oxford University Press, 1999.

Brinkley, Douglas. *American Heritage History of the United States.* New York: Viking Penguin, 1998.

de Tocqueville, Alexis. *Democracy in America. Reissue* ed. New York: Vintage, 1990.

Durant, John, and Otto Bettmann. *Pictorial History of American Sports: From Colonial Times to the Present.* Rev. ed. New York: A. S. Barnes and Co., Inc., 1965.

Holbrook, Stewart H. *Holy Old Mackinaw: A Natural History of the American Lumberjack.* New York: The MacMillan Co., 1961.

Hood, Adrienne D. *The Weaver's Craft: Cloth, Commerce, and Industry in Early Pennsylvania.* Philadelphia: University of Pennsylvania Press, 2003.

Klein, Philip S. and Ari Hoogenboom. *A History of Pennsylvania.* 2nd Ed. University Park, PA: Pennsylvania State University Press, 1980.

Leinbach, Paul W. *A Rich Family History.* Orlando, FL: Paul W. Leinbach, 1996.

Nash, Roderick Frazier. *Wilderness and the American Mind.* 4th ed. New Haven: Yale University Press, 2001.

Pennsylvania: A History of the Commonwealth. Edited by Randall M. Miller and William Pencak. University Park, PA: Pennsylvania State University Press and Pennsylvania Historical and Museum Commission, 2002.

Rich, M. B. *History of the First 100 Years in Woolrich.* Reprint ed. Salem, MA: Higginson Book Co., 2005.

Taber III, Thomas T. *Sunset Along Susquehanna Waters.* Muncy, PA: privately printed, 1972.

Treese, Lorett. *Railroads of Pennsylvania: Fragments of the Past in the Keystone Landscape.* Millersburg, PA: Stackpole Books, 2003.

Acknowledgments

This book was conceived by Tim Joseph, Woolrich director of marketing and media, and his assistance was of immeasurable value throughout the process of its writing and publishing. Special thanks to Teresa McCloskey of Woolrich, whose energy and enthusiasm were instrumental in tracking down photographs, arranging interviews, uncovering historical documents, and myriad other tasks. Numerous members of the Woolrich "family"—including past and present employees—gave freely of their time and shared their experiences. They include Charles Aides, Louise "Corky" Barnhart, Roswell Brayton, Jr., Lederle Eberhardt, Mindy Fisher, Marge Geise, Valerie Hallow, Bruce Heggenstaller, Rick Insley, Wade Judy, Vickie Laubscher, Leslie Noelk, Rick Osborne, Chester Pribble, John E. Rich, John Rich VI, Michael Rich, Jerry Rinder, Joann Rishel, and Roger Sheets.

Special thanks to Roswell Brayton, Sr. for providing us with the manuscript of his memoir, and to Paul W. Leinbach for sharing materials in his book *A Rich Family History*.

Thanks to Cathy and Dave Staples of Images Group for their vast knowledge of Woolrich and its history; to The Wild Studio for original photography and for the reproduction of historical documents; to Scott Sagar, curator of collections at the Thomas T. Taber Museum, Williamsport, Pennsylvania, for photographic research; to Grace Truax for her always able editing; to Barb Heggenstaller, Lisa Jo Smith, and Melinda Mathias-Porter for their excellent proofreading; and to Tom Turner for printing guidance.

Photo Credits

Photographs and illustrations are from Woolrich, with the exception of the following:

Pages 12: Keith Claxton illustration
Page 13, 15, 16, 17: From the collection of the Lycoming County Historical Society and Thomas T. Taber Museum
Page 20: Courtesy of William Maggs
Pages 43, 48: © Corbis
Page 45: Library of Congress, Prints and Photographs Division, Detroit Publishing Company Collection
Page 91: Doug Truax

About the Author

Doug Truax is a writer, editor, and publisher. He is the author of several books, including two children's books focused on the outdoors, and has written for several major outdoor companies. He is owner of Crofton Creek Press, a publishing company in northern Michigan. Doug puts his own collection of Woolrich gear to good use photographing wildlife and nature, fly fishing, hiking, and paddling on the small lake he lives beside.